The B e *Attitudes*

hes
e a
...You!

by BeBe

0 43422 69580 5

Written by Be Be
Cover Design by Design Dynamics
Typography by MarketForce, Inc., Burr Ridge, IL

Published by Great Quotations Publishing Co.,
Glendale Heights, IL

ISBN #1-56245-336-X

Library of Congress Catalog Number: 97-77652

Printed in U.S.A.

This book is dedicated to:

You!

INTRODUCTION

As a child, I heard my parents tell me to go to my room until I changed my attitude. "What did they mean by that," I often wondered. "What is an attitude? How can I change my attitude?" I usually found myself sitting in my room, mystified, waiting for my parents to change <u>their</u> attitude.

As an adult, I find that behaviors are a reflection of my mental approaches to life, i.e. attitudes. What I need in order to behave more successfully is a wardrobe of attractive, effective and positive attitudes. I now dress my mental self with attitudes of my choice.

I find that it's not necessarily *what* we think about but *how* we think about things that makes all the difference in the world. Free your mind from the fetters of fear which are the root of all negative attitudes.

Having this collection of "Be Attitudes" available to me over a long period of time has greatly influenced the quality of my life.

My outlook in general has improved, my relationships are more enjoyable and others find my attractive attitudes infectious. It rubs off on them. And, by the way, it's wonderful to live, work and play with people who have great attitudes.

This book contains treasures of positive attitudes from the English language. Thought-provoking phrases and sage advice follow each "Be-Attitude" to nurture your spirit and spark your imagination. Fill your mind with uplifting thoughts and embark upon a life journey of well being.

Step inside each one. Try them on. Feel the part. Experience the multitude of choices available to you at any given moment. Scan the selections often. Memorize them. Make up your own. Practice them. And positively accept being who you are, as you choose to be.

Be Able

Do for yourself all that you are capable of doing.
Only then will other people gladly assist you, should you
need further help.

Be Acting

The word "act" is the root word for the word PRACTICE.
It is the first step in making something happen.
But beware; it is also a kindred soul of REACTION.

BE ADEPT

Cultivate a refined sense of ability. Create confidence with your skills and talents. Seek to be first-rate and proficient.

BE AESTHETIC

Variety is essential to the concept of beauty. Take the contrasts you find in life and unify them with your sense of harmony.

Be Affable

The presence of a friend enhances enjoyment and promotes good will. Invite the opportunity to share affinities. Be likeable.

Be Affectionate

Touch another in a loving manner. Continue to attend your relationships with sincere, heart-felt endearments.

Be Affirmative

Establish your ideas with confidence and edify belief in the goodness you look forward to. Assert your worthiness.

Be Ageless

Live in the here & now. Do not restrict yourself to a chronological age.

BE ALLURING

Let your essence come forth and disclose irresistible appeal.
Arouse magnetic fascination with an attractively
charming personality.

BE ALTRUISTIC

Be thankful for those who gave their lives in order that you
could have a better chance than they had when they
were born. Always be concerned with the welfare of our
children's children.

BE AMAZED

Enjoy the surprise you feel upon finding the answers or solutions you seek. Take delight in what you find awe-inspiring. Marvel at the breathless wonders of life and the universe we live in.

BE AMBITIOUS

Be eager and bold to unleash the power of reaching for your dreams. Experience the passion of your enthusiasm.

Be Amiable

Be playfully loving in your personal relationships. Remain affectionate, easy-going and gentle.

Be Amusing

Elicit happiness with laughter and good-cheer, pleasantly and unexpectedly, bringing joy to others. Emanate the gentle lightness of life.

Be Appealing

Promote that which has real and eternal value within you. Garnish your attractiveness with truth, beauty and goodness.

Be Appreciative

That which you feel and show admiration for multiplies and grows more valuable over time. Escalate your worth and meaning, as you develop your mind.

Be Approachable

Be easy to talk with and pleasant to know.
Allow your unfolding personality to be
accessible with all of its emotions and intelligence.

Be Articulate

Present your ideas with clarity.
Formulate your thoughts and speak
your mind effectively. Learn to use
language easily and fluently.

Be Artistic

Show skill and excellence in all your art forms whatever they may be. Exhibit taste with discriminating judgment and sensitivity.

Be Asking

It isn't dumb to ask questions, but it would be dumb if you didn't. Don't be afraid to ask.

Be Assertive

Honestly promote your opinions and your actions by placing your footing on the firm ground of your self-esteem. Act in ways that enhance your self-respect and watch others respond accordingly.

Be Assisting

Be present in your life to give support and aid to someone else who needs it. Be available physically, emotionally and spiritually.

Be Attentive

Attention is a mental energy force. The success of your intentions depends on your ability to use this magnificent energy. Focus it.

Be Attractive

Produce pleasure and delight for yourself and those around you with a presence of beauty vibrating with appeal. Aesthetic forms and ideas decorate your body, mind and spirit according to your considerations of quality.

BE AUTHENTIC

Be genuine and real. Others will treat you as reliable and trustworthy and entitled to acceptance and belief because of your alignment with known facts and experience.

BE AUTONOMOUS

The one who conquers self has conquered the world. If you don't choose to do this others will do it for you. Operate under your own will power.

BE AVAILABLE

Be suitable and ready for use. Be present in your life for yourself and others. And be accessible emotionally, in order that it not be a lonely journey.

BE AWARE

Be mindful and knowledgeable, ready to respond to the known and the unknown. Consciously acknowledge your life and make the best of it.

Be Balanced

Great peace of mind can be attained when perspective has been adjusted to harmonious proportions. Stability is an ever-changing series of events, however, so remain ready to make adjustments.

Be Beautiful

That which is beautiful has excellence of form, color and presence. Beauty includes the noble and spiritual qualities of being you to the fullest.

Be Being

Be a human being, not a human doing or a human having. Possess the essence of personal presence.

Be Believing

Have confidence in the truth within you. And as you shine the light of your faith and intelligence, the truth will indeed set you free.

BE BENEVOLENT

Do good or cause good to be done. Be tender and loving in action and purpose. "Volant" means voluntary and "bene" means good. Be voluntarily good.

BE BETTER

You don't have to be sick to get better, because there is always room for improvement. Remember, not better than, just better.

Be Blessed

Be blissfully happy and contented, knowing that you are worthy of being happy. You were created to be this way.

Be Blooming

Unfold in your life like a flower. Allow yourself to establish your roots, find nourishment, create the structure of your stem, send forth your leaves to receive light, blossom exuberantly with the colors of your petals and smile!

Be Brain-Storming

Put your heads together. Develop new ideas with others and participate in solving problems with unrestrained discussions.

Be Bright

Be animated, lively and cheerful. First look to the light as the source of your being, and as you do so others will see it, too. You reflect that which you concentrate on. Polish yourself into a brilliant personality.

Be Brilliant

Find your talents and magnify them with
your participation.

Be Buoyant

In the great ocean of life, allow yourself to always rise
to the surface. Bounce back from disappointments and
depression and regain your posture.

Be Calm

Move serenely through your world and give permission for a tranquil solution to life's problems. Be a mirror for others, for through you they too gain a greater sense of peace of mind.

Be Candid

Remain open, sincere and spontaneous. Let your affairs be filled with heart-to-heart exchanges and genuine humor.

Be Cause

Be the cause for something, not just the effect. Choose to be the master of your destiny and the captain of your ship.

Be Centered

Drive your life as from the middle of your bliss. Be fueled with perspectives which balance the good and bad. Have a healthy approach to daily life.

Be Certain

That which you passionately want in your heart is truly possible. Be free from doubt and reservations.

Be Changing

Attend the present with an aptitude for modifying your identity toward a desirable future.

Be Charismatic

Exercise a remarkable drawing power over people without dictatorship. Inspire hope and confidence in the hearts of those you encounter.

Be Cheerful

Promote, express and induce a pleasant mirth when you are by yourself or with others. Embody a hearty inclination to work with optimism.

BE CLEVER

Show inventiveness and originality. Be mentally bright and utilize your intelligence. Be skillful in character.

BE COHESIVE

Be a force within the soul of humanity which acts to unite its parts.

BE COLORFUL

Flavor life with the spices of your personality. Be rich in your imagination. Display the rainbow-like spectrum of your personal attributes.

BE COMFORTING

Soothe and console the people you care about. Encourage them beyond these passing moments. Think of ways to help them do the things they cannot do for themselves.

Be Comical

Promote truly excellent causes and reasons for genuine laughter.

Be Committed

Entrust yourself to that which is worthy of you. Empower your relationships with the assurance of believable intentions.

Be Compassionate

Empathy desires the removal of the cause for pain
and suffering, for yourself as well as others.
Compassion emanates when you act on this desire.

Be Complimentary

As you express your opinions to others,
commend them constructively and foster
their self-esteem. Let your light shine.

BE CONFIDENT

Believe in yourself. Be assured that you are on firm ground.
Give yourself permission to be bold.

BE CONSCIENTIOUS

Have a sense of what is right or wrong in your conduct and
motives, impelling you toward right action.

BE CONSCIOUS

Be "with thought," aware of what you are doing, sensitive to the dialogue you are having with yourself.

BE CONSIDERATE

Deliberately contemplate and have regard for other people's feelings and circumstances.

Be Consistent

Steadfastly adhere to your integrated principles, motives, courses of action and forms of thought and feeling.

Be Consoling

Help to lessen other people's grief, sorrow and disappointments; re-establish a sense of solace and hope.

Be Constructive

Seek to improve the world around you with your actions, opinions and comments. You are responsible for building a future that can stand up to your criticism.

Be Cooperative

Be willing to work and act together for a common purpose, in harmony.

Be Courageous

*Be encouraged and know that the universe
supports your success.*

Be Creative

*Be original in your thinking and expressions.
Be ingenious with your imagination. Tap into
a pre-verbal frame of mind and feel your way into
notions which have never been before.*

Be Cultivating

Promote the growth and development of that which serves to bring success. Labor for the harvest of truth, beauty and goodness.

Be Curious

Be inquisitive, desiring to learn and know.

Be Daring

Have the necessary courage to be and do
something you desire.

Be Dauntless

Have purpose and fear nothing.
Your boldness is kindred to your genius.

Be Decisive

Engage your power of determination and display your ability to choose. Be free from ambiguity and hesitation. Resolve your determination to pursue your goals.

Be Delightful

Be responsible for the atmosphere you surround yourself with. Afford pleasure and happiness to those you love.

BE DESIRABLE

Be excellent and worth desiring. Be pleasing and fine for yourself first. Finish your posture with a smile.

BE DETERMINED

Be unwaveringly decided. Persist in your choices. Go for it.

BE DIFFERENT

Know that no one is identical and enjoy your distinctions.

BE DILIGENT

Be constant in your efforts to accomplish something.
Pursue your goals with persevering attention.

Be Discerning

Mentally distinguish the truth, beauty and goodness of your life.

Be Doing

Action is an integral part of being. Performance and execution are both important to manifesting your desires.

Be Dreaming

Indulge in your dreams and your aspirations.
Lucidly imagine a bright future and happy occasions.
Enhance your endeavors with visionary clarity.

Be Dynamic

Explode with enthusiasm and exude the
essence of activity. Empower your
self-esteem with effervescent emotions.

BE EASY

Let your disposition reflect an attitude of co-operation.
Get along with others and don't take things too seriously.

BE ECSTATIC

Let your emotions embrace and express the rapturous
delight you feel when all is right or becoming that way.

BE EDUCATED

Receive instruction from the schooling available by drawing upon your natural intelligence and willingness to learn. Let your teachers bring out the best in you.

BE EFFECTIVE

Whatever you set your mind to, produce the intended outcome. Burst forth with attractive results.

Be Elastic

Be capable of returning to your original self after being stretched, stressed and bent out of shape. Have a springy mental and physical constitution.

Be Eloquent

Exercise the power of fluent, forceful and appropriate speech.

Be Emancipated

Be freed from bondage or anything that would constrict your free movement. Be unconstrained by custom, tradition or superstition.

Be Empathetic

Be able to identify with the feelings, thoughts and attitudes of others. Your ability to sense the arena of life you are in will reveal many treasures.

Be Enchanting

Find delight within yourself. Keep focused on how things can be and instill these possibilities in others by example.

Be Endless

Enlarge the insight of your involvement in life. Expand upon your perception of eternity.

Be Energetic

Flip your switch on and exhibit spark and vitality with a childlike enthusiasm.

Be Engaging

Have a winning smile and a pleasing influence on others.

Be Enlightened

Possess intellectual and spiritual insight appropriate to the here and now.

Be Enraptured

Be moved to rapture; delighted beyond measure. Get caught up in the rhapsody of life.

Be Enterprising

Acquire initiative, ingenuity and energy.
Find a need and fill it.

Be Entertaining

Hold the attention of that which is agreeable
with that which is amusing. Know how to treat
your guests, as you would want to be treated.

Be Enthusiastic

Breathe life into your existence and let your purpose explode.

Be Evolving

Unfold over time. Become more of who you are by blending your possibilities into actualities in the process of becoming a new creation.

Be Excellent

Possess superior merit and be remarkably good.
Be instilled with outstanding qualities and matchless integrity.

Be Exceptional

Be more than what you would be if you didn't care,
and more than what you would be if you didn't try.

Be Exhilarating

Invigorate and stimulate pleasant, merry laughter, with good cheer and enthusiasm.

Be Expedient

Do what it takes to get the job done, without dragging your feet and without destroying or injuring anyone or anything in the process.

Be Expressive

Feel your thoughts as you speak and write. Enhance the effects of being heard with appropriate manners and gestures. Let your hands and eyes convey the emphasis.

Be Extraordinary

Be exceptional in character, and signify the remarkable.

BE FABULOUS

Be exceptionally good and unusual. Familiarize yourself with being marvelous, and recognize it when it happens for you. Blossom and be the incredible person you see you are.

BE FAIR

Play the game "I Win - You Win." Discover what it's like to be free from bias, dishonesty and injustice. Think before you act.

BE FAITHFUL

Be reliable, trustworthy and believable, in order to know the deep satisfaction of allegiance and affection. Be true to your words and keep your promises.

BE FEARLESS

Beckon that which is bold and brave within you. Reckon with that which you fear. Draw from the part of you which knows no fear. Be the Champion!

Be Feeling

Become acquainted with the non-thinking part of you. Know your heart. Give yourself permission for a capacity of emotions, especially for compassion.

Be Festive

When it's time to party, contribute to the joy of celebration. Dance and be happy.

Be Flexible

Be capable of being bent. Be pliable and be willing to yield.

Be Focused

Adjust whatever is necessary to become more clear and sharply defined. Your thinking, seeing, feeling, speaking and general being deserve to be managed with clarity.

Be Free

*Enjoy your personal rights and liberty,
and respect that for others.*

Be Friendly

*In order to have friends, be one. Send or leave notes
of cheer and good-will so people can know that
you're thinking well of them. Invite companions to
participate in your Odyssey of Life by sharing
significant experiences, hardships and insights.*

Be Fulfilled

Notice beauty and value in small things, as well as large. Embrace the people in your life with satisfaction and hold dear your achievements.

Be Fun

Provide enjoyment and happiness at work and play. Nourish your spirit with a sense of true pleasure. Frolic in the high spirits of freedom.

Be Gallant

Be elegant with your politeness and attention.
Free your high-spirited nature to exist. Rise to the
challenge of being noble.

Be Generous

Be free from meanness or smallness of mind or
character. Be liberal in the giving of your time,
talents and energy.

Be Genuine

Proceed as from the original stock, the original thought. Free yourself from pretense and deceit. Embrace the authentic you.

Be Glad

Attend your presence with all things positive. For everything bad there is something else good. Seek the light of happiness to dissolve the shadows of sadness.

BE GLOWING

Display the radiance of health, and let the rich colors of life show in your skin, your eyes and in your smile.

BE GRACIOUS

Show favor, tolerance and courtesy to others.
Be characterized by good taste.

BE GREAT

Be of high principle. Darkness cannot exist in the presence of light

BE GREGARIOUS

Enjoy meeting new people and developing your social network. Hang out with your friends and chew the fat with your family.

Be Happy

Contemplate thoughts which are delightful and pleasing. Be apt for joy and be felicitous through your actions, utterances and ideas. Have a propensity to laugh.

Be Harmonious

Help to form a pleasingly consistent wholeness. Be congruent and agreeable in your thoughts, feelings and actions, and create euphony within and around you.

Be Helpful

Be of service and quick to give assistance.

Be Honest

Signify the honorable in principles, intentions and actions. Be genuine and unadulterated. Show fairness and sincerity.

BE HOPEFUL

Hope is the life-blood of success, a close relative of faith.
It is what you believe in, but have not yet seen.

BE HOSPITABLE

Receive and treat guests and strangers as you would want to
be received and treated, warmly and generously.

BE HUMBLE

Allow neither praise nor slander to influence you. Know who you are but let others discover it for themselves.

BE HUMOROUS

Have a sense of humor. Do not take yourself so seriously that you cannot appreciate the music of laughter.

Be Idealistic

Pursue the concepts and things which you believe ought to be. Do not be trapped by what seems to be.

Be Imaginative

Foster your creativity and exploit your imagination. Investigate ways to free it.

Be Improvising

Be spontaneous. Act without previous preparation,
trusting your wisdom, instincts and insights.

Be Incomparable

Refrain from contrasting yourself with others.
The measure of all things is relative.
Possess your own set of standards.

Be Incredible

Inspire others with your life. Define your own path and do what you dream of doing.

Be Independent

Establish your own life and liberty. Rely on your own abilities and resources.

Be Ingenious

Look at things in a way no one else does.
Your clever solutions and resourceful
approaches make you a valuable associate.

Be Inquisitive

Knowledge is asking and finding.
Wisdom is willingness and discovery.
Experience is involvement and refinement.

Be Interested

Participate in activities which have the power to engage your curiosity. Display an attentiveness for what you desire.

Be Inventive

Create new products, ideas and techniques when you envision better methods and ideals. Act on your instincts to improve conditions, and have a propensity to be inspired.

Be Inviting

Offer friendship which is both attractive and alluring. Request the presence and participation of your family, friends and associates with a kind, courteous and complementary atmosphere.

Be Involved

Engage your interests and emotions with purposes you adopt. Get into the thick of it and contribute. Participate.

BE JAZZED

Choose to be alive and spirited. Approach life with an inclination for the off-beat and emulate the privilege to improvise.

BE JOYFUL

Be full of delight and express a thrill for life. Spread happiness and be of good cheer.

BE JUDGELESS

Suspend closure of your mind. Avoid forming inflexible judgements and unalterable opinions.

BE JUDICIOUS

Exercise your faculty of good judgement. Choose to be wise, sensible and well-advised.

Be Keen

Be highly sensitive and perceptive. Be enthusiastic in your endeavors and ardent in your dreams.

Be Kind

Preoccupy yourself with a loving disposition. Choose to be gracious and giving.

Be Kissable

Choose to be physically, mentally and spiritually attractive and beautiful.

Be Knowing

Embrace what you know, and enjoy the insight of this awareness. Give yourself credit for your experiences. Let wisdom guide your intuition.

BE LEADING

Be a leader with no one following you. Choose to prompt your own thinking and actions. Deduce your own set of values.

BE LEISURELY

Allow yourself to include the peace of relaxation in your routine of activities.

BE LIBERATED

Be set free from bondage and fear by releasing their grip on your attention. Prevail in a state of freedom.

BE LIEVE

"Lieve" is a word which means gladly and willingly desirous. It also means dear one, beloved and treasured. You are.

Be Light-Hearted

Be buoyant, upbeat and optimistic. Let your uplifting confidence permeate your surroundings.

Be Listening

Pay attention to others when conversing with them. Take note of what they are saying and, especially, of what they are not saying. Then, ask if your perceptions are correct.

Be Loving

Show affection and love. Express your affinities and good feelings as often as you like.

Be Luminous

Be an inspiration for others. Allow the truth to shine through you clearly and lucidly.

Be Magical

Use creatively diverse techniques to produce effects which render the ordinary amazing and remarkable. Enhance your life with the unique and unusual.

Be Magnetic

Display a strong, attractive power and charm. Position all of your positive thoughts and feelings up front. Repel negative forces with an optimistic mastery.

Be Magnificent

There is nothing so great that you cannot become it. There is nothing so grand that you cannot attain it.

Be Meditative

Take time to contemplate issues which matter most to you. Make your decisions with a clear mind. Shift gears by going through neutral first.

Be Meek

Be gentle and kind. Represent goodness and humility through your words and actions.

Be Merry

Be filled with cheerfulness and gaiety, joyous in your disposition. Let your spirit enjoy mirth on earth.

Be Mighty

Be exceptional in your strength of character.
Uphold truths and principles which act to promote
life, liberty and the pursuit of happiness.

Be Miracle-Minded

Believe in the miracles that take place in this world.
Appreciate being part of events in the physical world
which surpass all known human wherewithal.
Be open to what you do not understand.

BE MODEST

Be free from ostentation or showy extravagance. Temper your appetite with moderation.

BE MORAL

Be concerned with right conduct and principles. Conform to principle rather than to law or custom. Listen to your heart.

BE MOTIVATED

Tempt yourself to act by imagining how you will feel having accomplished your goals. Create your own incentives.

BE MYSELF

Above all else, be who you are. Get acquainted with all of yourself. Discern the "I Am."

Be Natural

Exist in accordance with patterns and principles of nature. Embrace the intrinsic value and constitution you were born with. Your essence contains the actual and the potential.

Be Neighborly

Show qualities befitting a neighbor. Overcome the tendency for isolation in life by being friendly, helpful and respectful. Encourage a sense of community. Promote friendship.

Be Nice

Be amiably pleasant, kind, desirable and delightful. Package and promote the best of yourself.

Be Nifty

Be clever and stylish. Be known for expressing your own unique place in the universe.

BE NOBLE

Constitute in your personality that which is of admirably high quality. Discern what is good and right. Follow your path, and it will lead you to a high regard for life.

BE NOURISHING

Supplement the body with good food and the mind with good thought. Strengthen the truth, beauty and richness within you by endorsing that which is worthy of you.

BE NOVEL

Choose to be relatively new and of a different kind.
Remain fresh and original.

BE NURTURING

Promote development and encourage the growth of your
body, mind and spirit. Offer a helping hand by sharing your
understanding and knowledge.

Be Observant

Be quick to notice and perceive. Pay attention to your surroundings, and keep your eyes on the road.

Be Open-Hearted

Be unreserved, candid and frank. Keep your love available with your personality, individuality and character in a seemingly impersonal world.

Be Open-Minded

Recognize how the processes of thinking and the contents of thought flow wonderfully when you are receptive to new ideas and arguments. Be unprejudiced in your perceptions.

Be Optimal

Be the best and most desirable you can be. Choose to orient yourself toward tasty results and rewards that are well worth it.

Be Optimistic

Possess a propensity of taking a favorable view. Reflect on your possibilities with hope. Be convinced.

Be Organized

Put yourself into a state of physical and mental competence and order, prepared to perform the task at hand. Know where things are.

Be Original

Belong to the beginning thought.
Connect yourself to that which is inventive
and creative. Allow this source to flow through
you, and sustain a fresh channel for new ideas.

Be Outstanding

Seek to be skillful with your talents.
Earn the prominence that will make you
pleasantly conspicuous.

Be Passionate

Embrace the strong feelings and intense emotions that are sparked within your soul and spread like wild-fire throughout your body. Breathe deeply and experience your ardent fever.

Be Patient

Be diligent in details which ensure success. Persevere through pain and discomfort, without complaint and anger.

Be Peaceful

Be inclined to avoid strife and dissension.
Proceed from a state of mind which is tranquil,
always seeking the path which promotes harmony.

Be Perceptive

Use your second sight. See without your eyes
and hear the inner voice. Let insight and
understanding guide you.

BE PERSEVERING

Persist in what you choose to undertake. Maintain a sense of purpose and sustain your dreams; they are the guiding light to your future.

BE PERSONABLE

Give others the gift of your warm ambiance and friendly charisma. Be likeable and outgoing.

BE PHYSICAL

Give your body the activity it needs to breathe and support the life you choose to embrace. Let your actions provide you with tangible experience.

BE PIONEERING

Be the first, be adventurous and be original in your pursuits. Pave the way for others.

Be Playful

Be able to take delight in pleasurable activities.
Release your frolicsome nature and let it bring you happiness.
Recapture the uninhibited part of your childhood and
get back in touch with your core being. Utilize this energy
to balance your life.

Be Pleasant

Be agreeable and enjoyable. Cultivate an
amiable personality, polite manners and a
social disposition.

Be Poetic

Endow your thoughts and expressions with a creative flair. Express from your heart the beauty and depth felt when to the essence of life you commit yourself.

Be Poised

Maintain a state of balance and equilibrium. Let your posture be composed with dignity. Carry your "Self" with assurance and confidence.

BE POSITIVE

Proceed in a direction which is potentially most beneficial and progressive. Emphasize that which is laudable, hopeful and desirable. Express an unconditional confidence.

BE POWERFUL

Within the constitution of your nature remember your personal history of strength and endurance. Command the attention of the people and resources needed by building on all that has brought you to this moment.

BE PREPARED

Put thoughts and matters into proper condition.
Maintain readiness and familiarize yourself with that which
is to be expected and unexpected.

BE PRODUCTIVE

Display powers of performance. Cause and bring about
the results you work for.

Be Professional

Polish yourself into the leader you dream to be. Maintain an attitude of being the best; willing to operate on a level commensurate with your abilities.

Be Progressive

Be one who advocates progress within technology, sociology and theology. Be forward thinking and excited about possibilities.

Be Prolific

Abundant productivity is within your capabilities. Produce liberally with care and efficiency.

Be Proportional

Size is relative; adjust your perspective to live in harmony and balance. Integrate body, mind and spirit with symmetry.

Be Prosperous

Handle your success, wealth and welfare with comfort. Acknowledge the richness of life and good fortune you deserve.

Be Proud

Think well of the accomplishments and character of yourself and others. Recognize quality and promote it. Be well-pleased.

Be Prudent

Be judicious and careful in your affairs.
Provide for the future by managing resources today.

Be Purposeful

Acquire a motive. Determine for yourself
what you want and take the steps to achieve it.

Be Quality

Demonstrate the highest character in both thought and action. Be conscious of your thinking. Enjoy the distinction of having attributes which are great, noble and excellent.

Be Questioning

Cultivate an alert and curious mind. Let your intellectual pursuits help you discover who you are, why things are the way they are and why you are here.

Be Radiant

An ambience of good health shines ever more brightly when you top it off with your smile. Emit rays of hope and joy.

Be Rational

You are endowed with the faculty of reasoning. Exercise it; show good judgment and "common" sense.

BE READY

Be prepared and in fit condition for immediate response and action. Don't hesitate. Be willing.

BE REAL

Have an actual, rather than an imaginary, existence. Choose to be genuine and authentic.

BE REASONABLE

Choose to be agreeable to and in accordance with reason, logic and insight. Be rational in your understandings and spice them up with appropriate feelings.

BE REBORN

Renew your existence through growth. Experience your own personal renaissance by letting go of who you think you are for who you think you can become.

Be Receptive

Be open to suggestions and ideas, able to access knowledge and inclined to intelligently admit mistakes as well as success.

Be Reciprocal

Be complementary in your affairs. Give, perform and feel in return with others. Decide upon an equal exchange in your relationships. Graduate from the theory of return-on-investment to a more supernal concept of mutually giving without the thought of return. Communicate.

Be Rejoicing

Choose to see good. Celebrate your blessings. Take delight in your associations and relationships, bringing joy to the lives of others through your own gladness.

Be Relaxed

Be free from the effects of tension and anxiety. Learn to let your body and mind let go of the demands placed on them. Re-energize yourself through rest.

BE RELIABLE

Choose to be trustworthy and predispose your character to be honest. Do what you say you're going to do.

BE REMARKABLE

Strive to be worthy of notice. Let your actions and appearance speak well of you and others will speak in like-kind.

BE RESILIENT

Choose to spring back from exhaustion, illness, depression and adversity. Resume your life with wholeness and purpose.

BE RESOLUTE

Make up your mind to make your dreams and visions come true. Be firmly resolved and determined.

Be Resourceful

Deal skillfully and promptly with new situations.
Use what is available to you to overcome difficulties
and solve problems.

Be Responsible

Be directly answerable for the effects of
your thoughts and actions. Accept the
consequences for what you cause to
bring about. Take ownership of your life.

Be Responsive

Allow yourself to hear, to feel, to think and to see.
Be ready to answer and reply within the spirit intended.

Be Rewarding

Remember to recognize results and acknowledge them,
whether they belong to you or someone else.

Be Rhythmic

Hear the music of your soul. Develop your sense of natural movement and timing of both body and mind.

Be Romantic

Subordinate form to content and encourage freedom of the heart. Express your emotions and celebrate nature. Partake in the adventure of love and the ideals of passion.

Be Savvy

Sharpen your perception and intuition. Be a step ahead. Know a lot but understand more.

Be Scintillating

Let your mind captivate others with its brilliance. Show your smile and ignite sparks of life in your eyes.

Be Secure

Choose to be free in your choices. Believe in yourself and be confident of your survival. Do whatever it takes to be safe, and then enjoy your privacy.

Be Seeing

Open your inner and outer eyes. Look around and watch, then perceive, in order to understand clearly.

Be Seeking

It is the question that leads to answers. Join the cycle of asking, searching and finding. Make requests.

Be Self-Assured

Trust in yourself and develop an internal dialogue of confidence. Be familiar with faith, reliance and positive certainty.

BE SELF-CONTROLLED

Exercise appropriate hold over your actions, feelings and emotions, recognizing, when it is most appropriate to let go.

BE SELF-ESTEEMED

Create personal value, and respect that only you can say who and how you are.

BE SENSITIVE

Open your heart and be in tune with other people. Treat their feelings with the same care and respect as you do your own.

BE SERENDIPITOUS

Seek that which is important to you to allow for synchronous discoveries. Enjoy making the connection.

Be Serene

Remain unruffled in the midst of the winds of human drama. Take counsel in the peaceful and the tranquil. Be fair and clear.

Be Sexy

Be exciting and enticing, enlisting all the depths of your person. Reveal the essence of your gender. Communicate your capacity for pleasure.

Be Sharp

Be mentally acute, alert and vigilant. The steering wheel is in your hands. Be a responsible driver.

Be Sharing

Pool your resources with others. Participate for better and worse, in sickness and in health.

BE SIGNIFICANT

Let the purpose of your life contain a remarkable kind of importance. Who you believe you are has consequences beyond belief.

BE SINCERE

Be genuine, free from deceit and hypocrisy, and enjoy the distinction of a meaningful life.

BE SOCIABLE

Be inclined to associate with others predisposed toward friendship. Between us there is so much to learn and enjoy.

BE SOULFUL

Know your soul; touch all the seeds of truth, beauty and goodness. Draw upon the deepest parts of yourself, and express the dance, art, music and literature that dwell within.

Be Special

Let yourself be distinct. Let yourself stand apart from others. The price of blending in is higher than being unique.

Be Spectacular

First impressions have a lasting effect. Display yourself dramatically and let your adventures be daring and thrilling.

Be Spiritual

Be motivated by love, activated by unselfish participation and dominated toward the ideals of truth, beauty and goodness. Awaken to the needs of others and be of assistance.

Be Splendid

Go beyond the ordinary. Let your qualities be magnificent and strikingly admirable.

Be Spontaneous

Have a propensity to express yourself in the moment. Say what needs to be said, when it needs to be said. Go forward in your movement.

Be Stellar

Sparkle like a star in your particular field of endeavor. Dwell on aspects and issues that have far reaching effects. Shine within the bubble of our universe.

Be Still

Learn the flow of time. Grow past survival into Being. Keep on keeping on.

Be Stimulating

Rouse others to action with encouragement. Incite effort with your own participation.

Be Striving

Exert yourself vigorously and apply yourself repetitively toward attaining your goals until you do.

Be Strong

Deliver results through use of great physical, mental and mechanical power. Apply your robust presence with both seen and unseen forces.

Be Studious

Investigate the nature and knowledge of your interests.
Examine and scrutinize all aspects. Be zealous
in your analysis.

Be Stupendous

Undertake that which has never been done before.
Accomplish what only dreamers can see. Be marvelous.

BE SUBJECTIVE

Engage your personality before you employ your impersonality. Objectivity is form, subjectivity is content. Glue your relationships together with a healthy balance of both.

BE SUBSTANTIAL

Let there be merit in your accomplishments, and let the effects of your life reveal true value. Weigh meanings in terms of what you know and understand.

BE SUBTLE

Be clever, skillful and ingenious. Deliver results which require mental acuteness and discerning penetration.

BE SUCCESSFUL

Acknowledge the accomplishments you've already achieved. Attend your life with an appreciation for attainment. Enjoy your rewards, prizes, honors and compliments.

Be Sunny

Applaud that which is cheerful and joyous.
Reflect the light of a happy outlook.

Be Supportive

Assist others, giving aid as part of a team.
Supply a loving attitude.

Be Sure

Let your mind attain a level of certainty which is free from doubt as to your reliability, character and actions. Be confident with what you expect.

Be Swell

Be a buddy to someone. Let your influence be timely and vital.

BE SWIFT

Be capable of moving with great speed. Respond quickly to opportunities and move with them. Be happening.

BE SYNERGISTIC

Let one plus one equal three. Work together and sanction a sum greater than its parts. A three-sided structure is the strongest foundation in our universe.

BE TACTFUL

Manifest a keen sense of what to do or say to avoid offending others. Be diplomatic.

BE TEACHABLE

Be capable of being taught; be open to instruction. Increase your net worth through guidance and training.

Be Tenacious

Hold fast to your beliefs. Train your mind to be highly retentive. Keep your identity together with a sense of purpose.

Be Tender

Express love and affection. Be easily moved to empathy and compassion.
Be gentle and sensitive.

Be Thankful

Admit your feelings of appreciation and express your gratitude. Let it edify your spirit.

Be Thinking

Let the river of thought fill your mind, and offer a rationale to life. Be careful in designing ideas with your mind. Ponder your opinions and refine your conjectures.

Be Thoughtful

Be given toward handling your life with consideration for others, as well as for yourself. Be mindful of the explosive nature of your contemplations. To think is to create.

Be Thrifty

Participate in a world of economics. Learn how to manage your personal economy. Make the most of your money. Make the most of your energy.

Be Timeless

Be restricted to no particular time.
Be part of the past as well as the future.

Be Tolerant

Have a predisposition toward endurance.
Support others as you would yourself wish
to be supported. Pardon inconveniences
with patience and understanding.

Be Tough

Be able to withstand hardships. Be resistant toward the mental and physical viruses which are ever present. Be tenacious.

Be Tranquil

Be free from lasting effects of disturbing emotions. Be free from the effects of commotion and tumultuous conditions. Seek balance.

Be Transcendental

Go beyond the ordinary limits. Surpass the expected, and clothe yourself with that which you feel you can become.

Be Triumphant

Rejoice over victory. Be exultant over the magnificence of success and justice. Enjoy the trophy.

Be True

Be faithful to the authentic in the best and most desirable sense. Reflect the sincerity of your feelings and intentions by allowing yourself to have basis in fact and action. Remain loyal to your word.

Be Trustworthy

Generate belief in you by others for your dependability and reliability by creating assurance of this in yourself.

BE UNAFRAID

Fear need not impair you. Let it bring your attention to the matter needing your awareness.

BE UNCONDITIONAL

Live your life without endlessly pre-qualifying requirements necessary for wholehearted participation. Let the sinews of your integrity support your sincerity.

U

Be Undaunted

Hold onto your vision firmly and clearly. Fuel your imagination with the inspiration of courage and valor.

Be Understanding

Demonstrate your ability to interpret information. Let your mind be engaged with reason, common sense and concepts which act to scaffold your awareness and appreciation.

Be Unique

Be incomparable. Stand alone in your own particular qualities. Cast your own shadow. Apply your own distinct characteristics as to how you are, what you do and how you do it.

Be Unlimited

Nothing is beyond you. Modify your thinking and feeling to include that which is boundless, infinite and vast within your creativity. Drink a glass of water and touch the endless river.

BE UNPREDICTABLE

Avoid falling into a rut by always moving toward the unqualified. Create and recreate.

BE UNUSUAL

Choose to be exceptional in character. Let your personality develop richly including that which is uncommon.

BE VALIANT

In the face of adversity enlist boldly courageous approaches and attitudes. Defend worthiness with excellence in action.

BE VERSATILE

Be capable of turning easily from one task to another; be cleverly adaptable. Let your skills have many applications.

Be Vibrant

Exude excitement in your personality. Affect others with self-assured energy. Be electric.

Be Vigilant

Maintain a careful observance for danger. Be mindful and take action to protect what you consider valuable.

Be Vigorous

Saturate your character with energetic vim and vitality. Choose to be active and robust. Be powerful and persuasive in your efforts.

Be Virtuous

Represent the best in human nature. Produce effects which result from pure motivations, modest assumptions and even temperament. Be morally excellent and chaste in your ethical principles.

Be Vivacious

Be lively and animated. Exuberate with the essence of life. Let your presence rejuvenate those around you.

Be Vivid

Be vibrant with life. Shimmer with exciting colors and a compelling presence. Breathe the freshness of life into yourself and others.

Be Warm

Enrich your journey with a friendly disposition. Act kindly and affectionately toward those you meet. Share your lively feelings with sincere emotions.

Be Well

Center yourself in the midst of all that is true, beautiful and good. Thrive wholeheartedly within the kingdom of Being.

Be Well-Balanced

Seek to exist in a state of equilibrium. See both cause and effect. Make the necessary adjustments and arrange your being into alignment with all that promotes life.

Be Well-Read

Expose yourself to the thoughts of others. Develop your imagination and educate your mind. Read as much as you can.

Be Well-Rounded

Pursue varied abilities and attainments. Become fully developed and maintain balance in your personality.

Be Well-Spoken

If your foot slips, you can recover from your fall.
If your tongue slips, you may never recover at all.
Express yourself carefully and with knowledgeable intent.

BE WILLING

Design your wishes and desires according to what you decide upon. Deliberately choose actions based upon intelligent reflection.

BE WIN-WIN

Participate for results that are mutual in reward. Prefer games and diversions where the aim is reciprocal.

VWX

BE WISE

Exercise your power of discernment and judgment. Know what is known to others and more. Choose with insight what you do today to create tomorrow.

BE WISHFUL

Imagine what its like to be, to do or to have what you long for. Aspire to ascend the circles of attainment. Ascribe perfection to yourself.

VWX

Be "With-It"

Get with the program and make it something it couldn't have been without you. Get on with your life.

Be Witty

Possess ingenuity in speech and writing. Permit your understanding to be amusingly clever in perception and expression.

VWX

Be You

You are the "I AM" within you. Your memory, understanding and insight make up your identity.

Be Youthful

Embrace a wholesome enjoyment of freshness and vigor. Enliven yourself with the eternal qualities of innocence, curiosity and vitality.

BE ZANY

Emphasize your personality with dramatic humor. Add a sense of fun to your self-image, and seek to surprise others with an unexpectedly good nature.

BE ZEALOUS

Express your passions and devote your intelligence to diligent efforts.

BE GIVING

Supply copies of this book to your friends, families and associates. Share the illuminating treasures found within, and bequeath these mentally enriching heirlooms of thought to your children through example.

BE INVITED

Submit comments and personal stories of positive attitudes to: Be Be, 6925 1/2 W. 14th Avenue, Lakewood, CO 80215.

<u>Other Titles by Great Quotations</u>

201 Best Things Ever Said
The ABC's of Parenting
African-American Wisdom
As A Cat Thinketh
Astrology for Cats
The Be-Attitudes
The Best of Friends
The Birthday Astrologer
Chicken Soup
Chocoholic Reasonettes
The Cornerstones of Success
Daddy & Me
Fantastic Father,
   Dependable Dad
For Mother, A Bouquet
   of Sentiments
Global Wisdom
Golden Years, Golden Words
Grandma, I Love You
Growing Up in Toyland
Happiness Is Found Along
   the Way
High Anxieties
Hollywords

Hooked on Golf
I Didn't Do It
Ignorance is Bliss
In Celebration of Women
Inspirations
Interior Design for Idiots
I'm Not Over the Hill
The Lemonade Handbook
Let's Talk Decorating
Life's Lessons
Life's Simple Pleasures
A Lifetime of Love
A Light Heart Lives Long
Midwest Wisdom
Mommy & Me
Mrs. Aesop's Fables
Mother, I Love You
Motivating Quotes
   for Motivated People
Mrs. Murphy's Laws
Mrs. Webster's Dictionary
My Daughter,
   My Special Friend
Only a Sister

The Other Species
Parenting 101
The Perfect Man
Reflections
Romantic Rhapsody
The Rose Mystique
The Secret Language of Men
The Secret Language
   of Women
The Secrets in Your Face
The Secrets in Your Name
Social Disgraces
Some Things Never Change
The Sports Page
Sports Widow
Stress or Sanity
A Teacher Is Better Than
   Two Books
TeenAge of Insanity
Thanks from the Heart
Things You'll Learn...
Wedding Wonders
Words From the Coach
Working Woman's World

GREAT QUOTATIONS PUBLISHING COMPANY
Glendale Heights, IL 60139
Phone (630) 582-2800 • Fax (630) 582-2813